Little Angels

Little Angels

MQP

There is always one
moment in childhood
when the door opens
and lets the future in.

Graham Greene

No one has yet fully realized
the wealth of sympathy,
kindness, and generosity
hidden in the soul of a child.

Emma Goldman

Every child begins the world again, to some extent, and loves to stay outdoors, even in wet and cold.

Henry David Thoreau

The child begins life as a pleasure-seeking animal.

Selma H. Fraiberg

Double your pleasure. Double your fun.

Wrigley's Doublemint chewing gum advertising slogan

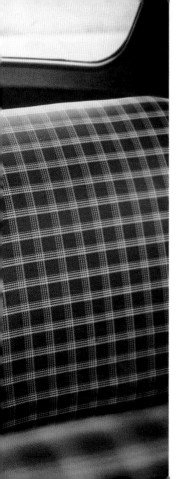

There are two classes
of travel—first class,
and with children.

Robert Benchley

Childhood is a forgotten journey.

Jean de la Varenne

Do engine drivers, I wonder, eternally wish they were small boys?

Brian O'Nolan

The best way to keep children's clothes clean for several days is to keep them off the child.

Leopold Fechtner

Where there's a will there's a way, and where there's a child there's a will.

Marcelene Cox

Another tumble!
That's his precious
nose!

Thomas Hood

Children are unaccountable
little creatures.

Katherine Mansfield

Children and chickens
would ever be eating.

Thomas Tusser

Even when freshly washed and relieved of all obvious confections, children tend to be sticky.

Fran Lebowitz

One must ask children and birds how cherries and strawberries taste.

Johann Wolfgang von Goethe

A child is always
hungry all over.

Charles Dudley Warner

All encounters with children
are touched with social
embarrassment.

Sylvia Townsend Warner

A child should always say what's
    true,
And speak when he is spoken to,
And behave mannerly at table:
At least, as far as he is able.

R.L. Stevenson

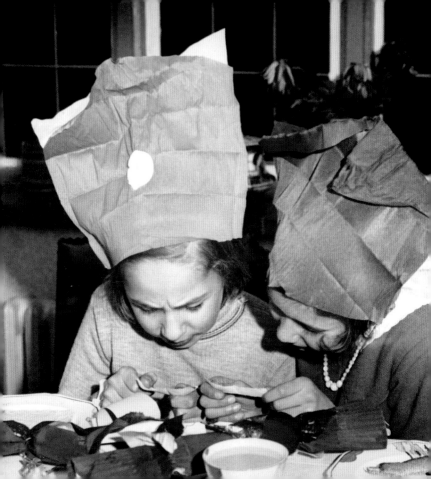

A child who is not rigorously
instructed in the matter of table
manners is a child whose future
is being dealt with cavalierly. A
person who makes an admiral's
hat out of linen napkins is not
going to be in wild social
demand.

Fran Lebowitz

41

Do you like children?
  I do if they're properly cooked.

Alison Skipworth and W.C. Fields

The beginnings of
altruism can be seen
in children as early as
the age of two.

Neil Kurshan

Children always take the line
of most persistence.

Marcelene Cox

The most effective kind of education is that a child should play amongst lovely things.

Plato

Our child appeals
To the cultivated mind.

Ogden Nash

One for mommy.
One for baby . . .

Anonymous

The age of a child is inversely correlated with the size of animals it prefers.

Desmond Morris

Little girls are cute and small only to adults. To one another they are not cute. They are life-sized.

Margaret Atwood

It should be noted that children at play are not merely playing; their games should be seen as their most serious actions.

Michel de Montaigne

The wildest colts make
the best horses.

Plutarch

Teach us delight in simple things,
And mirth that has no bitter springs.

Rudyard Kipling

Childhood's a risk we all take.

David Hughes

At three, four, five, and even six years the childish nature will require sports.

Plato

Boys like romantic tales; but babies like realistic tales— because they find them romantic.

G.K. Chesterton

Children who play life
discern its true law.

Henry David Thoreau

Children are natural mimics who act like their parents despite every effort to teach them good manners.

Anonymous

In their sympathies, children
feel nearer animals than adults.

Jessamyn West

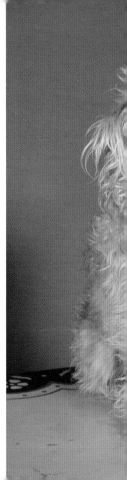

Let the children in our
    care
Clean their shoes and
    comb their hair;
Come to school on time
    —and neat,
Blow their noses, wipe
    their feet...
Let them, please, say
    "drew", not "drawed";
Let them know the
    answers, Lord!

Allan Ahlberg

There is not an agent in the CIA or the KGB who knows how to conceal the theft of food, how to fake being asleep, or how to forge a parent's signature like a child.

Bill Cosby

Don't forget that compared to a grownup person every baby is a genius.

May Sarton

There's only one pretty child in the world, and every mother has it.

Proverb

Don't you like children?
  No. They always seem to be so wise.

Janet Margolin and Woody Allen

There is nothing like dream
to create the future.

Victor Hugo

I seem, for my own part, to see the benevolence of the Deity more clearly in the pleasures of very young children than in anything in the world.

William Paley

Who can fortell for
what high cause
This darling of the
gods was born?

Andrew Marvell

Between the wish and the
thing life lies waiting.

Unknown

What are so mysterious as the eyes of a child?

Phyllis Bottome

Very young people are true but not resounding instruments.

Elizabeth Bowen

All God's Chillun
Got Rhythm.

Gus Kahn

Prodigy: a child who plays the piano when he ought to be in bed.

J.B. Morton

How inimitably graceful children are in general before they learn to dance!

Samuel Taylor Coleridge

My music is best
understood by
children and animals.

Igor Stravinsky

A child's attitude towards everything is an artist's attitude.

Willa Cather

Youth would be an
ideal state if it came a
little later in life.

Herbert Asquith

Picture Credits

Cover: Fairy anointment, circa 1935. p. 4/5: Kite flying, 1955. p. 6/7: Share it out, 1949. p. 8/9: Wet and wild, circa 1935. p. 10/11: River bathers, 1948. p. 12/13: Matching tots, circa 1960. p. 14/15: Nearly there yet?, 1953. p. 16/17: Engine driver, 1936. p. 18/19: Room for a little one, 1973. p. 20/21: Two little pigs, 1952. p. 22/23: What handicap?, 1917. p. 24/25: Playtime, 1966. p. 26/27: Children by pool, 1968. p. 28/29: Young chef, circa 1935. p. 30/31: Drying off, 1935. p. 32/33: Blackberry kids, 1943. p. 34/35: Lunchtime, 1932. p. 36/37: Mini naturist, 1947. p. 38/39: Hot cross buns, 1937. p. 40/41: I don't get it, circa 1959. p. 42/43: Fridge raider girl, circa 1955. p. 44/45: Open wide, 1945. p. 46/47: Checker twins, 1955. p. 48/49: Bunny hug, 1932. p. 50/51: Hospital reading, 1954. p. 52/53: Junior Chef, 1954. p. 54/55: Girl's best friend, 1935. p. 56/57: Waiting to go, 1935. p. 58/59: Ears are useful, 1937. p. 60/61: Little jockey, 1970. p. 62/63: Teddy bearettes, 1935. p. 64/65: Skiing twins, 1940. p. 66/67: Kick and run, circa 1968. p. 68/69: I can read, circa 1950. p. 70/71: Bear wash, 1938. p. 72/73: Playing grownups, 1937. p. 74/75: Rin Tin Tin reader, 1955. p. 76/77: FSA nursery, 1942. p. 78/79: Working hard, 1935. p. 80/81: Nappy girl, 1944. p. 82/83: Schooldays, 1955. p. 84/85: Watchful faces, 1958. p. 86/87: Young angel, 1954. p. 88/89: Fancy dress, 1954. p. 90/91: Toddler grooming, 1941. p. 92/93: Bedtime prayers, circa 1950. p. 94/95: Little girl with cat, 1973. p. 96/97: Music hath charms, 1938. p. 98/99: Cockney ding dong, 1941. p. 100/101: Piano lesson, 1949. p. 102/103: Cutsey curtsey, 1960. p. 104/105: Playing records, 1935. p. 106/107: The rosebuds, 1934. p. 108/109: Sombrero kids, 1948.

Text Credits

p. 4/5 Excerpt from *The Power and the Glory* by Graham Greene, reissued by Penguin USA, 1995. p. 6/7 Excerpt from *Living My Life* by Emma Goldman, Dover Publications, 1970. p. 10/11: Excerpt from *The Magic Years* by Selma H. Fraiberg, reissue by Scribner, 1996. p. 12/13: Wrigley's gum advertisement. p. 14/15: Excerpt from *5000 One and Two Line Jokes* by Leopold Fletcher, HarperCollins, 1986. pp. 30/31 and 40/41: Excerpt from *The Fran Lebowitz Reader* by Fran Lebowitz, Vintage, 1994. p. 36/37: Excerpt from *The Museum of Cheats* by Sylvia Townsend Warner, Viking Press, 1947. p. 44/43: Dialogue from "Tillie and Gus" (Paramount Studios; screenwriter Walter DeLeon and Francis Martin). p. 44/45: Excerpt from *Raising Your Child to Be a Mensch* by Neil Kurshan, Atheneum, 1987. p. 50/51: Excerpt from *Candy is Dandy* by Ogden Nash, Carlton Books Limited, 1994. p. 54/55: Excerpt from *A Dictionary of Contemporary Quotations*, compiled by Jonathan Green, Pan Macmillan, 1982 (Desmond Morris © quote). p. 62/63: Excerpt from *The Children's Song* by Rudyard Kipling, Anchor Books; reprint 1988. p. 64/65: Excerpt from *The Pork Butcher* by David Hughes, Schocken Books, 1985. p. 68/69: Excerpt from *Orthodoxy* by G.K. Chesterton, Image Books; reissue 1991. p. 74/75: Excerpt from *I Really Lived* by Jessamyn West, Viking Press, 1982. p. 76/77: Excerpt from *The Puffin Book of Utterly Brilliant Poetry* by Brian Patten, Penguin, 1998 (poem © Allan Ahlberg) p.78/79: Excerpt from *Fatherhood* by Bill Cosby, Berkley Pub Group; reissue edition 1994. p. 80/81: Excerpt from *Mrs. Stevens Hears the Mermaids Singing*, W.W. Norton & Company; reissue edition 1993. p. 84/85: Dialogue from "Take the Money and Run," (Anchor Bay Entertainment, 1969; screenwriters: Woody Allen and Mickey Rose). p. 96/97: Excerpt from *The Death of the Heart* by Elizabeth Bowen, Knopf, 1939. p. 98/99: "All God's Chillun Got Rhythm," Song lyrics and title by Walter Jurmann, Gus Kahn, and Bronislaw Kaper, EMI Robbins Catalog, Inc. Robbins Catalog, Inc./Gus Kahn Music Co. p. 106/107: Excerpt from *The Song of the Lark* by Willa Cather, Mariner Books; Reprint edition, 1983.